A True Story

Collateral Damage

Corruption, Lies, and Deceptions

MICHAEL J. KUCHERA, JR.

DocUmount Publishing *Diversified*
244 5th Avenue
Suite 3-209
NY, NY 10001
646-233-4568
www.DocUmountPublishing.com

DPd
publishing

Published by
DP Diversified
a division of DocUmeant Publishing

244 5th Avenue, Suite G-200
NY, NY 10001
646-233-4366

Editor: Anne C. Jacob

Cover Design and Layout by Ginger Marks, DocUmeant Designs
www.DocUmeantDesigns.com

ISBN: 9781957832135 (print)
ISBN: 9781957832142 (digital)

Library of Congress Number: 2023945924

Dedication

Thank you to

My family for their patience.

My senator from Florida, who was the only government person willing to help me.

Victor Tranquillo, CPA and friend, thank you for your help.

Anne C. Jacob, my editor and proofreader for her great job.

Deceased

Jerome Lawrence Rinzel, Tax Attorney and Consultant, Wauwatosa, Wisconsin, your genius maneuvers gave me time, but your letter and all our evidence meant nothing. Thank you for trying.

Attorney Ralph Talarigo, Author of the one and only Kuchera Industries Inc.

This is my only formal documentation that I own the company, and I never sold any stock to anyone.

Contents

Dedication iii

Introduction vii

Chapter 1: The Search for a Satisfying Career 1

Chapter 2: Saved by the Flood 8

Chapter 3: Virginia 12

Chapter 4: The Birth of Kuchera Industries, Inc. 16

Chapter 5: Science, Technology, and Politics
The Illegal Purchase and Takeover of K.I.I. 22

Chapter 6: Bankruptcy and Bin Laden 31

Chapter 7: Serving the Elite The "Wonderful" IRS . . . 34

Chapter 8: Health Issues 43

Chapter 9: After Years of Searching 45

Epilogue 49

Introduction

ONE DOES NOT become CEO of a corporation overnight. Therefore, I felt it necessary to describe my long and varied career leading up to owning the company that would eventually destroy my life. As you journey with me through this book, I invite you, the reader, to tour each consecutive job and the highlights of my multifaceted professional endeavors.

I am determined to make others aware of how an honest citizen attempting to clear up a tax problem was targeted, pursued, and wronged by an IRS agent. Let this book serve as a warning to entrepreneurs and honest businessmen. Be on the lookout for problems caused by government agencies and criminal activities, even among friends and family members.

⚬══◆══⚬

My name is Michael J. Kuchera, Jr. I was born in a small coal-mining town in Pennsylvania. My father was a coal miner, and my mother was a stay-at-home mom. I had two older brothers. Growing up, I attended a one-room schoolhouse, overcame dyslexia, and played sports in high school. My family and I were church-goers. In 1958, I married my high school sweetheart, Rosemarie.

In 2003, Rosemarie and I retired to Florida, hoping to rebuild our lives and live peacefully in the Sunshine State. We could never have anticipated how an honest attempt to run a legitimate contract manufacturing company, followed by what should have been a tranquil retirement, would develop into a series of harrowing ordeals created by dishonest business associates, corrupt government employees, and backstabbing, criminal family members.

The wrongs committed toward us are detailed in this book. Over the years, I have kept copious records of every communication, event, and incident, including original copies of legal documents. Other than medical records, there is no paper trail of the undue physical and psychological damage that my wife and I have endured.

Chapter 1: The Search for a Satisfying Career

To dream the impossible dream, that is my quest. — Cervantes, *Don Quixote*

FROM THE TIME I began working, I have been motivated by the unknown human drive to move on from a plethora of experiences, always looking for something better. Consequently, my jobs were many and varied. Although I was impressed with the function and operation of each company, becoming a permanent part of any one of them was never an option, nor was it my choice.

Each new job contributed to my eagerness to absorb knowledge. As I discovered and developed proficiency in the required skills, my increasing desire to learn something new inevitably led to seeking and accepting other job opportunities. According to my wife, I am a visionary. Now, I invite you to join me on a tour of the early days of working and my quest for a fulfilling career.

My association with Ladish Company in Cudahy, WI, was a great experience. It was one of the largest drop-forging companies in the world. They housed a drop-forge hammer and press large enough to fit a car underneath. I was able to observe the evolution of the product from the forge shop to the machine shop. This company made the first nose cone for NASA rockets.

It was impressive to see all the processes necessary to build the product. My work there was an invaluable experience that took place during a historic moment in our country's rocket-building timeline. I was extremely fortunate to have seen a red-hot piece of metal that looked like a huge doughnut rolled out to make a twenty-foot wide, three-foot high, and one-foot-thick ring, which was a perfect circle.

While at Ladish, I worked in every inspection job they had. Although I enjoyed the jobs, the process to keep a job or move forward became intolerable. After years of putting up with the policy of bidding on jobs to procure my next position in the inspection department, I left.

At American Motors in Kenosha, WI, I observed a large-scale complicated production process, which was the assembly line. Seeing all the planning necessary to make everything come out right was extraordinary. My first job was to check under the hood — all connections and gas lines — to make sure they were tight. I did one side of the hood, and a partner on the other side did the same. We did our job, but every once in a while, a gas line would look and feel tight, but it wasn't, so when the car was started, it would catch fire. This was always an astonishing event. The line was moving at six hundred cars in eight hours, or seventy-five cars an hour, so one had to keep moving.

Eventually, I went from the final inspection to the motor division to the floor sweepers, where I had endless sleep time. I read every book I could, like Lincoln, Hawaii, Henry David Thoreau, Michener, Socrates, Plato,

Jung, etc. This company failed long after I left, but I could see why.

From there, I became the assistant manager of a finance company in Kenosha, WI, where I soon realized that once you borrowed, you were stuck there forever. I did everything I could to show this cruel cycle to many poor people. I also learned that, according to federal banking regulations, there are preset guidelines for the operation and disbursement of funds.

I was responsible for balancing the daily accounts and monitoring all the businesses we serviced by floor planning their inventory. This responsibility gave me a working knowledge of the banking world. To make extra money, we would leave the office at five and drive to contact the customers when we couldn't reach them at home on the phone during the day.

Some of the stories I was told were very sad, and some were funny. I will never forget meeting a grandfather at his home, and when I addressed him as Mr. X, I followed with, "I heard you died." He said, "What? Again?" then we laughed.

The manager of this loan company was a pleasant person. Unfortunately, he was asked to go to Michigan and run a bank, which was a better job with better pay. His replacement was a man from hell, and he made our lives miserable. He fired me for going to night school twice a week after five o'clock, and I was certainly happy to leave that job.

My new job was working in a Midland Industrial Paint Company laboratory. The building was across the railroad tracks on the shore of the mighty banks of Lake Michigan. This interesting factory produced specialty paints for many unique products. One product was a coating utilized on the electrodes of transformers. This special coating emitted fumes that deterred insects and prevented their accumulation on the transformers.

Some of the workers were gifted with matching paint colors. It was a real art. On every floor of the factory, there was a small room set off to the side of the five-hundred-gallon containers of the various paints which were constantly being mixed. The techs would keep a constant eye on the color by bringing samples of the paint to us, and we would check it for various specifications—for color and correct mix. You can't make mistakes while working on a five-hundred-gallon tank of paint.

The lab I worked in had a large sliding door that separated it from the manufacturing area. From my lab window, I could see the small windows of rooms on the side of the factory, where my coworkers would also be doing various checks on the constantly mixing paint. One day, I saw a window blow out of a small room due to the worker not following safety measures, and the worker blew out with it. The large fire door was closed, and the fire company was there in minutes, but a train was blocking them from getting to us. We were evacuated and helplessly left standing on the shoreline of the lake. I left the paint company for several good reasons. The company made an excellent product, but the location on the other side of the tracks was far from a choice property, it was unsafe.

My next job was working for a company that serviced hospital television systems. The TVs would break down, often requiring a completely new set. My job was to go into the rooms where the TV was reported as not working and put in a new TV. Carrying the small sets from the room to the truck and back was simple but tiring.

I became so good at carrying the TV sets from the rooms to the truck that I was given a second hospital to service. By three o'clock each day, I would have the truck full and return to the center. Then I would repair the units and use them as spares. The company imagined I should be able to fix as many as fifteen TVs in a couple of hours, but this was an unrealistic expectation.

In every room, the patient would control the audio speaker system for the television with the same device they used to call the nurse. The patient communication system became a problem, and I was told to repair it. To my surprise, I was shown the switching network, and it was enclosed in a metal shield that was all one piece. I finally got it open, and it clearly had instructions to call the company for repair service, which meant that the company should be called and I should go no further with repairs.

The highlight of this endeavor was when a handsome fourteen-year-old boy dying of cancer needed an antenna to get a particular baseball channel that wasn't on the hospital group network. I told my boss, and he was happy to get me an antenna and cable. I put the antenna on the hospital roof and ran the wires to his room so that he could watch the game. This single accomplishment made my stay at this company worth my time, despite being a part-time student and the unrealistic timeline expectations of the company.

Still in Kenosha, WI, I was employed at Snap-on Tool Research and Development (R&D) Lab. This large company made diagnostic equipment for the automobile industry. At first, I worked in the drafting department, but after a year, I was asked to work in the electronics department.

There, my project was to build a timing light to replace the antiquated one being used. I worked for years trying to redesign a circuit out of the radio handbook to do what I needed it to do. I finally succeeded in accomplishing my goal: to make the circuit do what I wanted it to do.

My second project was a tach dwell meter. This circuit had to count the cycles a car engine makes at different speeds on four, six, and eight-cylinder engines and keep the six-inch meter stable, or else it would shake and give incorrect readings. It took another few years, but again, I succeeded.

These products had to be triggered by our new capacitor pick-up method. I was the inventor of these two devices. They were the first solid-state timing light and tach dwell meter; my name is on both patents.

During that time, I also collaborated with several universities in the pursuit of developing a gas analyzer to measure automobile emissions for a pollution control device, which the state of California eventually adopted.

While I was at Snap-On, I became involved with the Snap-On Credit Union. My efforts included a lobbying tour of industries throughout Kenosha, Wisconsin, to obtain credit union reforms. This endeavor was instrumental in securing the legislation for credit unions to have customer checking accounts, which came to fruition in the 1960s.

In 1970, I asked the vice president of the research and development laboratory for a raise in pay and was told that, although I had already invented two items, I didn't have my degree yet. In fact, of their eight engineers, I was the only one who had produced anything. So, I left after six years and two inventions of two new products.

The VP's comment about my lack of a degree was ironic since I had been attending night school for fourteen years while working full-time and raising a family. During this time, I attended the Milwaukee School of Engineering (MSOE), St. Francis College, Northern Virginia College, Elizabethtown College, Mount Aloysius College, Union Grove Teachers College, and Dominican College. I participated in job-related seminars and workshops, which are too numerous to list but would amount to hundreds of hours. I had all the tools I needed to work as an electrical engineer. I finally ran out of time to finish my BA degree, but it no longer mattered, since I now had the necessary knowledge.

Apart from my professional career, I also have an honorable discharge from the United States Army and worked with the Boy Scouts of America as a regional director.

In all these jobs and experiences, I became tolerant of repetition and honestly enjoyed each one. This concept is an integral part of our giant society of working people.

Chapter 2: Saved by the Flood

There is a tide in the affairs of men, which, taken at the flood,
leads on to fortune. —Shakespeare, *Julius Caesar*

IN 1971, I relocated to my hometown of Portage, PA, where
I began running Portage Electronics, a TV sales and repair
center. I had successfully repaired a color TV while we
were still in Wisconsin, and this, combined with the skills
gleaned from my years of night school at MSOE and experience repairing hospital TVs, led my wife to suggest this
new business venture.

At first, it was fun, but I soon discovered that the
diagnostic time per unit took too long to be profitable.
Fortunately for me, the tubes in the television sets were
built so flimsily that they burned out and needed to be
replaced frequently. Without these poorly built break-
downs, making money would have been impossible.

Now in PA, with a son and a daughter, my wife got
us to sponsor a local Girl Scout troop. We became so
involved that we took our group to Independence Hall in
Philadelphia for the two-hundredth birthday of our country in 1976. We also traveled to Mount Vernon, the home
of our first President. We were able to take these trips and

do many activities with our Girl Scout Troop by selling candy. Many of our girls had never had the opportunity to go on such trips or stay in a motel, and were delighted to participate in this new experience.

Even though I did not have much spare time, I sponsored and coached a little league baseball team. One of my most memorable moments came when I was the only coach who showed up for a game one day, so I asked all the young boys who came to practice every week but sat on the bench what position they would like to play today. We lost the game, but, for once, the young boys, the faithful ones, finally had an opportunity to play in a position they always wanted. After the game, I treated them all to ice cream. Fun times!

I was also active as a religious instructor in my local church. I acted as a spokesman for different groups and was chosen to represent many organizations for local and national government issues. Once again, just as I had done with the Boy Scouts in 1960, I found myself contributing a substantial amount of time to the welfare and development of the children in my community. Each opportunity allowed me to make personal contact with companies throughout the United States and abroad.

Several years later, my brother Bill became interested in moving back to PA and wanted to open a bar near my store. He and his family had been living in South Milwaukee for many years. With the assistance of Ralph Talarigo, a personal friend of mine from our high school days who was now an attorney, I was instrumental in finding an available bar.

My brother Bill purchased the old bar across the street from my store, and his two sons, Bill Jr. (Billy) and Ronnie, ran it. I would bar tend for him occasionally if needed. We had fun and helped one another when necessary. Billy did a great job organizing stock and ordering supplies for everyday sales. The bar became well known, and young people from the area flocked to it.

Still relying on the power supply burnouts to make money in the TV repair business, I added appliances. Mr. Jones, a wise banker, warned me not to take this step, but I did not heed his advice. In a town of only about 4500 people, there was not enough of a market to compete with the large-volume discount appliance stores and shopping malls.

When the appliance truck arrived in front of my store expecting me to sell the whole truck's worth, I said, "Take your truck and get the hell out of here!" They did—and immediately severed our business relationship. At that point, I knew I had to do something else. My TV and appliance store had made me a living, but the distributor had made me poor.

On the evening of July 19, 1977, Rosemarie was driving home from working her three to eleven shift at the hospital in downtown Johnstown. The rising water levels and pouring rain made driving almost impossible, but she had to get home. She made it across the bridge just as the water began flooding the street. She crossed another road, and seconds later, it collapsed into the muddy water.

As soon as Rosemarie reached the end of town, the dam broke. A few hours later, the entire road was washed away. She recalls, "It was like I was going, and everything collapsed behind me. The devastation was following me. I never saw such lightning and rain. The flood destroyed everything." The notorious Johnstown flood had begun, and Rosemarie had escaped its wrath with only moments to spare.

My store and my brother's bar were completely ruined in the 1977 Johnstown flood. He and his sons moved back to Wisconsin, and I lost track of them. The flood was a gift from God. My wife was safe. As far as my business was concerned, I had to do something else. The flood forced me to move on whether I wanted to or not.

Chapter 3: Virginia

You have power over your mind, not outside events. Realize this, and you will find strength. —Marcus Aurelius, *Meditations*

WITH MY BUSINESS destroyed and a family to support, I began sending out resumes. Jobs in the Johnstown area were scarce, even nonexistent. Several college graduates from the area had migrated to Maryland or Virginia to find employment, and I now found myself making the same decision. Years ago, I had read about a small community in Reston, VA, that was built to house people who worked in one of the many high-tech industries in that area, so I focused my job search energies there.

In 1980, I received a call from PRC Reality Systems out of McLain, VA, and accepted a job as a system analyst, which meant I would be relocating. Rosemarie was able to hold down the home front by herself and was busy tending to her eighty-four-year-old mother's needs, and my son and daughter were away at college, so I moved into a small apartment and made the four-hour drive back home to PA every weekend.

At forty-six years old, I did not mind temporarily living away from home. In fact, I was quite happy concentrating on myself for five days a week. My routine was to work late, jog after work, make a simple dinner, and sit on my patio on the ground floor of the apartment I was renting. For relaxation, I took up meditation and became quite good at it.

My first project as a system analyst was to repair a light display system that a programmer designed, used microchips, and was hardwired to display a light system on a large map of the USA. At any time, the president or a company officer could look at the large display and see

Michael Kuchera, Jr., data communications supervisor, examines reconditioned multiple listing computer terminal at PRC Realty Systems' service facility near Dulles International Airport in northern Virginia. With 14,000 PRC terminals in use by real estate brokers, Dulles facility plays important customer service role by repairing and reconditioning several hundred terminals each month.

a solid light, which stood for an up-and-running system, or a blinking light, meaning it was down but being repaired. All 180 branches were represented. This map was imperative since any non-working unit would cost the company six hundred dollars per hour. After that repair, I was asked to work in the network control center to fix problems in the Hewlett-Packard (HP) Octal brain center field.

After a year, I was transferred to the PRC Dulles Repair Center, which was where all the equipment came in from around the country to be repaired. During that time, I set high standards for excellence and was so valuable to the company that I was featured in the yearly *Shareholder's Report* magazine. Over one hundred representatives from across the United States regularly came to the Dulles facility for training, which I provided. I taught personnel how to maintain an assortment of complex computer and communication equipment the company utilized. Northern Virginia College recognized this program and issued a one-credit certificate to complete the course. When I took a course in programming at the college, the professor asked me to teach the class during the hardware section of the course, so I did. Not surprisingly, I received an 'A' in the course.

While at the repair center, I became aware that the transition to microchip manufacturing was about to take off and that there would be a future market for microchip technology. Eventually, it would replace through-hole technology. The motherboard of the HP mainframe was populated with all kinds of microchips. I also noticed that we were trashing older modems and equipment that we once would have repaired.

Driving home every weekend was a lot of work, and I realized I now had the knowledge, skills, and ability to do what God wanted me to do—to start my own business. So, I left the job in Virginia and moved back to Pennsylvania to begin work on my own.

Chapter 4: The Birth of Kuchera Industries, Inc.

*Two roads diverged in a wood and I — I took the
one less traveled by. —Robert Frost*

WORKING FOR PRC Reality Systems in Virginia, first as a
systems specialist in network control and then as a supervisor of the repair center, I saw a future in surface mount
technology. When I returned home to Pennsylvania,
I realized that the larger companies were not yet set up to
meet this need, and I thought, "Wow! There's gonna be
like a trillion dollars worth of work in this thing when I get
in!" My background was in electrical engineering, and
I was confident I had the skills and knowledge to take the
leap into running my own business.

I worked my tail off and started Kuchera Industries
Incorporated (K.I.I.) to quickly procure capital for my
microchip ambition. I was the founder, president, and
owner of K.I.I.. I surmised that I had a ten-year window
for my surface-mount technology to be in demand before
the major companies could develop their own facilities.

Concurrently, I realized that large communications
companies like PRC also needed to purchase extremely
costly specialty cables. I surmised that building these

specialty cables would be a lucrative method to make startup capital for my new company. I set up an area in my basement and taught my son, Michael Kuchera, and younger nephew, Ron, how to assemble the cable jobs. We could purchase the equipment needed to complete the hand-soldering jobs with the profit from assembling the cables.

The basement would not suffice if we wanted our business to grow. While my son searched for a place to house the new business, I was driving to Maryland several times a week to visit different companies and look for a business that had jobs simple enough for us to handle. Michael procured a small, rented facility in Johnstown, PA, which we leased from Mr. Jerry Leaser. Our first hand-soldering job was for a company named TTC, out of Gaithersburg, Maryland.

At this time, after ten years of having no communication with my brother or his family, Ron's older brother, my nephew, William Jr. (Billy), came to my house and told me he heard I was starting a business, and that he would like to work with me and be my partner. We had worked together years earlier when he owned the bar, so his visit was not strange. However, he was living in Wisconsin, and we had not communicated in years, so it surprised me that he knew about my plans.

Before I could make sense of the situation, Billy said, "I have to tell you a secret, though. See what you think of it."

We went for a little walk, and he said he had been in prison on a dope charge. He asked me to promise not to tell anyone, and I agreed to keep his secret. After all, he was family, and many young people were getting into that type of thing. Although I did not share his values, I did feel compelled to take him in and help him start on a new path.

At this juncture, doing the hand soldering, I now had a small group of workers to complete the TTC job, and my nephew, Billy, got right to work on a bench with the group. On this first job, we had to hand-clean the residue from the solder off of the finished boards. We used freon, which was great for washing the flux off the boards, but hard on the hands.

We obviously needed a freon drip tank to wash the boards after soldering. I found one, along with a wave soldering machine, both used, but working, and Billy found the guy who would lease these machines to us. So, we drove down to Columbia, MD, and rented a truck there. We had it loaded with the items and drove home. I arranged to pay for these machines as long as they worked, and the company agreed.

The machines were in our shop area when I got to work the next day. I had previously made arrangements for the electrician to get us wired for 440. Still, I was impressed with the expeditious manner that Billy had gotten the machines up and running when I expected them to still be on the truck.

For a while, Billy stayed in Wisconsin, working on selling his store and a very large boat. I personally saw the boat and store when I went to his sister's wedding. At the time, I was also surprised to find the large house that my brother had acquired. I really thought this visit would turn out to be the start of a new and better relationship between us. My decision to become fifty-fifty partners and form a sub-S corporation with William Jr. was made with compassion and the hope that he would get a second chance to rectify his mistakes.

Billy and I worked very well together during the early days at K.I.I.. He was an outstanding plant manager, and I was excellent at obtaining business. I was always on the road, and he ran the shop. I often took him with me to introduce him to people in various companies. My intention was to further develop a personal relationship with our customers so that when we got a job from them, Billy could talk with these people. It was at this time I noticed Billy was getting frustrated by his lack of technological prowess, but I could not argue with his success. He had acquired many connections and was able to procure the equipment we needed.

I traveled to Maryland, West Virginia, Virginia, Delaware, and Washington, DC, to pick up job kits from my customers to take them to my facility. Every kit was inspected, and the customer was notified of any missing parts before we began to assemble the kit. At first, I personally checked every board, then delivered the finished product.

Our customers were major companies in the emerging electronics industries. They included Versitron, Cryptek, Arbitron, Aiken Advanced Systems, and Optelicom. I always took the time to visit Fairchild, Raytheon, HP, and IBM on every trip.

As the company progressed, I required a high-speed pick-and-place machine and a microwave oven (Vitronics). Getting them was not an easy task. A lot of hard work went into it, and after six months, we were able to purchase what we needed. The graphic read-out on all the jobs was a comfort to our customers and insurance for the company.

We needed a faster turnaround time in assembling through-hole boards, so I created the *pyramid stuffing rack*. This device enabled us to complete the jobs faster than any of our competitors. I hired my brother to build the pyramid racks for the board stuffers. In addition, he built rails for the placement of chips on the pick-and-place machine, which he graciously did at a much-reduced price. I also purchased a used thirty-six-inch milling machine.

My brother helped do other important jobs, including making the tables static-free. We used the belts from the coal mines and had them cleaned. I was proud of my brother's innovative talent — I would give him a drawing of just about anything, and he would build it.

I was working on getting our first microchip job from Versitron. It was a Department of Defense (DOD) job. Versitron qualified us for this job, so I purchased a used pick-and-place machine prototype for ten thousand dollars to do a million-dollar job. The company was happy to get rid of it, as operators were hard to find. After a month, we could not work fast enough for all the calls for our machine.

While running K.I.I., I evaluated every job, and my company displayed its excellence of workmanship to the highest level. I always delivered the finished product to our customers personally, and this resulted in receiving additional jobs. We only grew from there. When delivering a job, I constantly looked for other sources. I would visit the shipping docks of a new prospect to learn more about the company.

Our workmanship and honesty were a magnet to large companies. We were unchallenged, and our name sold the company. I never took advantage of any of my customers or the companies I serviced. Because of all of these factors put together, the business flourished. It went so fast and grew so quickly that we evolved from only needing a workplace the size of a small room to occupying the whole building. It grew from four to three hundred people.

As far as I was concerned, I was proud that K.I.I. had become a true American success story, with the family doing business together and successfully acquiring the Department of Defense and other government-related contracts.

Chapter 5: Science, Technology, and Politics

THE ILLEGAL PURCHASE AND TAKEOVER OF K.I.I.

When modern men and women lost religious faith, they lost the asso-ciated belief that human beings are special, that we were created with purpose to undertake a life with meaning. Science, technology, and politics have not yet filled that void and probably never will be able to do so. —Dean Koontz, foreword to *Invasion of the Body Snatchers*

AT FIRST, HAVING several relatives work for me seemed like a fantastic idea. My nephews were great and continued to be for years. We thoroughly enjoyed our success at building the company and working together. There was no reason to suspect that anything was wrong. When I asked to have something done, they were on it.

Things changed in 1990 and worsened through 1993, making the last three years of my tenure at K.I.I. hellish. During these diabolical years, my nephews and brother teamed up to destroy me mentally. They used all the tricks of their felonious natures to bring me down. I became perplexed and appalled that my good name was being maligned by those I trusted—the same people I had hired and trusted to run the office and take care of the books while I searched for and found companies that would flood us with work.

The grave reality of my situation came to light when my nephew, William, approached me with a new contract. It was a proposition to make my nephews and their father, William Sr., partners with me, and it would give them seventy-five percent of the company.

I told him to get real and go to hell. Being presented with this shocking, unfair contract was the first time I felt strange about hiring family members. After all, I intended to include them in the business's future success and was proud of their efforts. Now, as president and CEO of the company, this abrupt attempt at getting me to sign a contract put me in an awkward situation and aroused my suspicions. I was appalled by what I learned about the people I had trusted.

One evening, the family had left for the day, and I began looking at the books. I discovered that multiple nefarious, fraudulent activities and cheating on DOD contracts had been going on for several years. To make a bad situation even worse, they had literally taken over the company, and, without my knowledge, it had become a sub-S corporation belonging to them. According to these books, I was an "employee" with no status or position—as a CEO, I just didn't exist.

Unbeknownst to me, while I was traveling from state to state to provide the personalized service that our customers had come to expect, my nephews were manipulating me into a treacherous position and leaning toward more activities that were not a part of my ethics.

Bill was deeply involved with the political lobbyists, and that influence made him realize that more money could be made with less work. His interest went in that direction, and I wasn't part of that plan. I began to piece together how these events had transpired to make me lose complete control of the company, and I was horrified at the emerging plot to replace me.

K.I.I. was doing all of the manufacturing work for Cryptek, a startup company in Herndon, VA. When I saw their product, I was impressed, so I helped them to get started by doing some work for them. I was right—they became a big customer for me as they grew.

GKI was a government-related company from Johnstown that dealt only with DOD contracts. GKI had acquired Cryptek in the international case, GKI vs. Ricoh, based on a non-compliance issue with the "Buy America Act of 1934." GKI had built large parts for the military and now decided to venture into the electronics world. This move proved to be a mistake, for they didn't do any quality research on this entirely different industry. My involvement with the case helped to save Cryptek and GKI from going bankrupt when the Defense Commercial Communications Office (DECCO) ruled in their favor in a multi-million-dollar contract.

At this point, in addition to three hundred partially assembled fax machines from Cryptek, I also had a million-dollar job with Arbitron Ratings Co. We were flooded with complex diagnostic equipment to test each unit after assembly. During testing, I found more problems that should have been addressed before the build was attempted. Finally, GKI had so many financial overrides that they decided to sell Cryptek.

In my eagerness to maintain a strong working relationship with the company, I carried them for four hundred thousand dollars, saving them from bankruptcy. Carl Sax, from GKI, had a working relationship with the new owners, and we finally made arrangements for repayment. However, Cryptek was slow to repay us, and we went on half-salary. I had no choice but to finish their debacle of their unfinished machines. The company's buyer cooperated with me, and I finally got paid.

On many occasions, in my travels, I heard comments from engineers about the unethical nature of my nephew, and several of them were even participating in these practices. My nephews did not share my morals or ethical principles and had been making deals over the phone with these people.

I was appalled when I learned that Peter Whorly, a man who had been caught in a dope deal and put in prison with my nephew, William, had given my company five thousand dollars when I was first starting my business. William was on the phone with him every day. I later learned that he was caught in another dope deal and was again sentenced to prison, this time for twenty years.

William told me he planned to take the 5 percent he verbally promised Mr. Whorly because "Peter will never live through twenty years of prison."

I replied, "Like hell, you put that money in an account for the dumb ass, for someday he will need it."

In a final attempt to find a way to fix the company without bad publicity, I needed to find another attorney. I spoke with Victor Tranquillo, a CPA, who verified that

I was being cheated. Then the realization hit me that, with all of the nefarious activities that had been occurring without my knowledge, I had to make a choice—the company or me.

William was running the company's every function, including the money and the shop, while I was in the field servicing our prolific assortment of customers. He found a small computer company in Cleveland, Ohio, and told me that he was going to service this company himself. Although I warned him that this was a poor choice, he ignored me and started to do some business with them. Eventually, this company went bankrupt, and we lost at least $100,000.00.

My nephews and my brother, William Sr., really started turning the screws on me, saying things like, "Why don't you retire? You can't handle it anymore." I was on the road when Ron called me and said I needed sixty thousand dollars to pay my taxes. In all the time we were in business, I never recalled signing a form and believed the company had paid all the taxes. My decision to leave the bookkeeping in the hands of others had been the wrong choice.

I called the IRS and asked for a copy of the K.I.I. taxes for the years I had run the company. They told me there were no taxes paid by Kuchera Industries Incorporated for those years. My nephews did the same thing with the federal government. They manipulated the title so there would be no record of a company.

One day, William said, "Mike, we are killing ourselves. I'm going to get out of this business and move to Florida." He proceeded to inform me that he found Mr. Jim Dudiak, who had a large company similar to ours in Pittsburg, PA, who would buy our company because he needed to expand quickly. I was skeptical but interested. He explained, "It is a perfect sale scenario. Carl Sax of GKI is familiar with the due diligence thing." He had a selling price in a few days, and I thought this would be the end of my three-year nightmare.

About a week later, we conducted the sale in the office of Mr. Dennis McGlynn, my company attorney. By this time, I was so mixed up that I was easy prey. When I saw the contract, I said, "I don't see Jim Dudiak's name." William noted that Mr. Dudiak wanted to get the deal over with today. He had arranged to call Mr. Dudiak to let him know to put the check in the bank after I signed the contract. When I questioned Mr. McGlenn, the attorney, about whether or not this was a binding contract, he said, "I wish someone would give me a deal like that. You could write it on a rock, and it would be valid."

That day, my floor manager, Thomas Breu, informed me he had just gotten off the phone with James Dudiak, who had a $100,000.00 check for me. Unfortunately, this was only a lie that William had set up. Tom found out very soon that his lie meant nothing to William because years later, I learned that he was gone from the company shortly after this performance.

My nephew insisted on staying on for a year to make a smooth transition. I offered to stay with him, but he convinced me to leave. I asked if everyone working for the company would stay, and he confirmed they would. I asked about the new owner and was told he had many government contracts, and our company would continue to grow.

With all of the questionable activity, I decided to speak with Mike Sossong, a friendly attorney. He inquired about my reason for selling, and I told him not to ask. He wanted to get a rap sheet on William so we could know more about his life and previous run-ins with the law. I told him not to do it because I would have a bigger problem if William found out. He persisted, reminding me that he was an officer of the courts and had the right to see William's record.

I honestly think Mr. Sossong was trying to help me, but the next day, William was furious with me. I did not know why until I discovered he had an underground network reporting to him about everything. A friend of his wife worked at the sheriff's office and had told him that Mike Sossong had called for the report. In my opinion, this was not only unethical but an unlawful act by the sheriff's office employee.

According to my company lawyer, K.I.I. was allegedly sold on February 10, 1993. I was shocked. After ten years of hard work, suffering from health issues due to the long hours and extensive driving, and struggling to maintain my sanity after learning about the unethical activities that had taken place, I decided that I had no choice but to leave the company. After I left, the former manager of GKI became a VP in K.I.I..

I ran the company from 1983 to 1993 and would come to regret leaving the bookkeeping to others. There was no turning back or explanations to justify this dangerous, legal predicament that my family had left me in.

The last thing I did before leaving the company was to sign some papers that had something to do with not taking advantage of the new owner's pension plan. Although I did not trust William, I had complete trust in Ron, and

I didn't think the new owners should be required to contribute their profits to my plan.

Contrary to his word, William never left the company, and Mr. James Dudiak, the alleged buyer of my company, claimed to have changed his mind. I am positive his checking account increased by a large cash deposit on the day of the alleged sale.

I lost track of Peter Whorley for many years, since he had been in prison. Now, he had gotten out of prison early and was suing my nephew for his percentage of the profit in Kuchera Ind. Inc. for the startup money he had given him. Although William had told me that it was five thousand dollars, Peter informed me that it had been fifty thousand, and now he wanted me to represent the truth about the deal he had made with William Jr.

Poor Mr. Whorley never had a chance. My nephews were rich with all the money they had stolen from me and were above a simple, truthful statement. I went to the trial. When I read the transcript, it showed how well-rehearsed my nephews were. As I walked out of the court, Peter asked, "Don't you want to say hello to your nephews?"

I stopped and glanced to my left where they were hiding. They both ran up to me and hugged me. I stood in shock, for this was such a foreign thing for them to do, but now the act was so significant. They would do anything to protect the money.

After that, I talked to Peter, and he told me that the dope deal he had been put in jail for was paid for from my office by Ronald and William Jr. How low can a person get? A good barometer would be my nephew.

Twenty-four years later, I started looking for the pension money I had invested in the original company's plan. After three years of searching, I discovered I had once again been the victim of my nephews' deceptions. In addition to exempting the new owners from contributing to my pension, the papers I had signed also called for the money already in my plan to be taken out and placed into a bank as an IRA.

The money went into PNC Bank, but the bank never informed me of this account. My nephews had decided to take the last crumb from me. With further investigation, I discovered that William Jr. had begun making the arrangements to take me out of the plan a month before I left. The hasty agreement signed by William and Ronald Kuchera was uncalled for. Our good friend and in-house notary, Judith Plummer, would sign anything we put before her. She trusted us all and had no idea what my nephews were up to.

My well-meaning effort to reform them had failed, but at least I gave it a good try.

The end of this chapter brings us to the beginning of a lifelong pursuit of justice.

Chapter 6: Bankruptcy and Bin Laden

How do you go bankrupt? Two ways. Gradually, then suddenly. — Ernest Hemingway, *The Sun Also Rises*

LEAVING KUCHERA INDUSTRIES in the hands of corrupt family members in 1993, I thought I had completely removed myself from the situation and that anything that happened to the company from then on would be their problem. I planned to have no communication or involvement with the new owners.

Thinking out of the box, I invested in a small pizza business and a coal truck. The coal truck driver was the husband of the woman who ran the pizza shop, and I was glad to provide jobs for their family. However, they were not business people, and I eventually found that they were cheating me out of my profits, and I had lost $50,000.00. Once again, it was time for me to move on.

In 1995, four other people, two companies, and I formed GLM (God Leads Me) Enterprises Company. They needed a leader and nominated me for the position. Our project concepts were varied, and we needed to secure funding to bring each one to fruition.

Rather than using one of the fifteen hundred landfills in our country, one of our successful projects was a fusion method that burned any type of garbage. Waste management companies used it in several states to replace landfills, and it is still being used today.

Another project I envisioned was a battery charging unit on one of the mountains we planned to purchase in California. It would electronically charge batteries on satellites, and I planned to rent the land I had purchased. That was my vision. I'm a visionary.

My favorite project was an aqua-hydroponics, vegetable farm, and fish farm under the same roof. It would be a tremendous second business for the farmers. Each farm would have a large building containing a fish farm. The water from the fish would feed the plants—beautiful vegetable gardens with tomatoes growing twenty feet high!

On April 4, 1997, a heart attack stopped all of my activities. I had to go to rehab for three months and was unable to work for almost a year. I requested a payoff from K.I.I. and even offered my nephews a payoff discount of eighty-five thousand dollars from my money from the sale.

After recuperating, I again focused on GLM funding. I invested the buyout money in a deal with Wisconsin attorneys Foley and Lardner and their England counterparts, Nicholson and Graham, the Bank of Boston, and the Bank of London. Lloyds of London originally insured this deal.

We had an opportunity to be financed through the World Trading System. In anticipation of a successful meeting, I used all my personal funds to complete the necessary paperwork for a trip to London, England, which would help us secure the funds. Rosemarie was excited to purchase clothes for our trip, and I was thrilled that we had been accepted into the world money program. Unfortunately, that trip never happened. Suddenly, the project was closed.

Osama Bin Laden used this same program to make money for his terrorist groups. I lost my fee and thousands of dollars in attorney fees and travel expenses. We had the backing of an onshore and offshore group of attorneys who controlled the financing of this program under strict government regulations; therefore, the program would be open again in a year. However, it was financially impossible for me to wait so long for it to open.

Later in 1998, the IRS informed us that we owed taxes for 1997, which I later learned was due to an erroneous Form 1099 filed by K.I.I.. If this form had been corrected, it would have shown that we had no tax due. I had lost money on the buyout. There was also a procedural error because I did not send my Form 1045 in a separate envelope but included it with the tax documents. I was unaware of this at the time.

My tax attorney insisted that we owed nothing, but K.I.I. refused to comply with my attorney's requests for information without a subpoena. We were not able to get the documentation that we needed to put an end to this financial nightmare.

Although GLM never went bankrupt, in 2000, I personally filed for bankruptcy in Pennsylvania. My funds were gone, and there was no hope of getting the money I needed. We lost our cars, my home in PA was sold in a sheriff's sale, and we moved to Maryland. My wife and I worked in Maryland for several years. Then we moved to Florida.

Chapter 7:
Serving the Elite
THE "WONDERFUL" IRS

Communism and Fascism are the obvious examples of ideolo-
gies that not merely devalued the individual but denied legitimacy
to the very idea that the masses exist for any purpose other than
to serve an elite and to die for the philosophies of that elite.
—Dean Koontz, foreword to *Invasion of the Body Snatchers*

FROM 1997 TO 2007, we replied to all communications
from the IRS and complied with all information requests.
We were living in Florida and surviving off of our Social
Security checks. Then, in July 2007, the IRS levied our
Social Security checks for $1556.10. With an earnest
desire to ensure that this complicated situation would be
resolved in the best way possible, we employed JK Harris
Co., a group specializing in tax issues, to help us. My son
and daughter helped me pay the $1500 fee for this service.

While we were waiting for a response from them, on
October 11, 2007, I received a letter from the Cambria
County Courthouse in Ebensburg, PA, stating there was
an overage of $29,358.81 from the sheriff's sale of my
Pennsylvania house in 2000 being held in escrow and that
I should apply for it, which I did. It seemed that our finan-
cial situation might be improving.

Even better news arrived on November 16, 2007, when we received a letter from the JK Harris Co. stating:

We are pleased to inform you that we have success-fully placed your account in an "Uncollectible Status" with the Internal Revenue Service. . . . Since your account is currently uncollectible, your contract with our company has been satisfied and we are closing your file. We wish you all the luck in the future.

They had successfully established that we were CNC (Cannot Comply) and our income was insufficient to pay. After four months of being levied, the levies were stopped. The CNC notification should have been the end of the entire issue. However, this was the start of yet another harrowing financial ordeal.

In September 2008, the IRS started to levy our Social Security checks. Jerry Rinzel, my tax attorney, and I were puzzled about where to look for an error in the past tax forms or anything to explain this sudden madness. In October, I had to sell my car to have enough money to pay our rent.

During this pursuit, JK Harris Inc. discovered that I had a federal tax lien in my name at the courthouse in Pennsylvania and that it would expire on November 16, 2008. JK Harris advised me to wait thirty days and then call to have it removed since it would be ten years old. They gave me an IRS number to call.

I called on December 8, 2008, and after speaking to several different people, I was directed to Mr. Batdorff, who reluctantly referred me to Mr. Steve Kovscek of the technical services department. Kovscek seemed to be try-ing to scare us and menacingly told me and my wife, "You will never get the overage at the courthouse in Ebensburg, and furthermore, I will renew the lien forever."

These statements by an IRS Agent were uncalled for, unprofessional, and appalling to me. He then proceeded to put liens from several states on our property in Pennsylvania. This prevented us from doing business in any of those states. He treated us like we were criminals.

December 31, 2008, started like any other New Year's Eve, but at 6:30 PM, there was a knock at the door. I was being served a federal court summons from none other than Steve Kovscek. This single event was devastating to my wife and bewildering to me. *Why would someone serve a summons at 6:30 PM on New Year's Eve? Why now? Why us?*

My wife and I were required to go to the Ocala Courthouse to deliver documents showing that I owed no taxes for 1997. We had difficulty walking from the parking lot to the main entrance. I was 73 at the time, with a degenerative hip, and my wife was 70, with bad knees. We literally hobbled, helping each other walk, and compliantly delivered the documents.

We were unaware at the time that the IRS and FBI were planning to raid my old company on January 1, 2009.[1] I began to connect the dots only after I learned of this event. The clerk's subpoena on December 31, 2008, at 6:30 PM, made it look like I was included in the raid to take place the following day. I also learned that he was the one who had levied our Social Security checks. Details of this raid, which had nothing to do with me, were later made public in this Washington Post article from January 2009.[2]

On January 15, 2009, I was informed that the IRS, FBI, and ATF had raided Kuchera Industries, Inc. and the homes of my nephews. Subsequently, Kuchera Industries Inc. was refused all future government contracts and was forced to sell to API Technologies for fourteen million dollars in cash and ten million in stock. My nephews were waiting to be indicted by the federal government.

Several months later, I received a call from a Washington Post staff writer, Carol Leonnig, who informed me that she had read the deposition that I gave to the court when I was asked by my nephew's "best friend" (Peter Whorley) to support his plea for the money he was owed.

She had spoken with Mr. Dudiak, the alleged buyer of K.I.I., who told her he knew of Kuchera Industries, Inc., but had never spoken with or even met with Bill Kuchera and was not involved in the sale of the company. This news excited her since she was writing an article about the company's ties to Pennsylvania congressman John P. Murtha.

At that time, Murtha was the chairman of the House Appropriations defense subcommittee. The Navy had suspended my nephews' company from future contracts so that an investigation could occur. Unaware of the extent of the investigation and the political and personal ramifications, I agreed to an interview.

In this interview, I told all of the events that took place, and Mr. Jim Dudiak, the supposed buyer, was interviewed by her. Incredulously, she reiterated that he had insisted he was never involved in the sale of K.I.I.. I later sent a letter to him asking for the truth, and I received a threatening letter from William's attorney in return. The sale had been fraudulent, and Dudaik turned out to be a front for my nephews to obtain control of the company.

I also told her that Bill and Ron had tricked me into selling the business to a shell corporation they secretly controlled, and she included my statement in the article.

I also told her that since I had given Bill a fresh start and made him my partner, I honestly believed him when he told me he had found a local buyer. But I later learned that this was not the case.

According to Investigative Reporter, Carol D. Leonnig, of the Washington Post, Jim

Dudiak, the supposed buyer of Kuchera Industries, Inc. in 1993, knew of KII, but never

spoke with or had any meetings with Bill Kuchera of KII. Ms. Leonnig interviewed Mr.

Dudiak and he confirmed that he never spoke with Bill Kuchera about buying Kuchera

Industries.

To confirm this statement, you may contact her:
Carol D. Leonnig
National Staff Writer
Government Accountability Team
The Washington Post
▓▓▓▓▓▓▓▓▓▓▓▓▓▓▓▓▓

Above information by Michael J. Kuchera, Jr.

June 9, 2011

Michael J. Kuchera Jr. ▓▓▓▓
▓▓▓▓▓▓▓▓▓▓▓▓▓▓▓▓▓▓▓▓▓▓▓▓

I have a 1997 tax issue that an agent of the IRS decided to pursue
I was forced to dig into my tax archives along with my then tax
Consultant to disprove this action.
After 4 years of intensive research I found via Taxpayer Advocate
Service and was informed of a missing Form 1045 from my Tax file.
Then a Federal Court ruled that the Form 1040X for 1997 and the
Form 1045 and all the supporting evidence for the 1998 and the 1999
Tax Forms were propertied.
An investigation of the fraudulent 1099 that was issued by Kuchera
Industries Inc. in 1997 was never addressed, even after an extensive
explanation was submitted in the returns.
Kuchera Industries Inc. was raided by the IRS, ATF, and FBI and was
forced to sell the company for $24 million plus.

Agencies I contacted.

Tax Advocate Service
Douglas Shulman IRS commissioner
Merlene Burnham Chief Commissioner's Correspondence
Mary Ellen Kim IRS Chief Counsel.
IRS Office Chief Legal Counsel, (CC:GLS:CLP) Washington ,DC
Erick Holder US Attorney General

People I asked to help me.

Senator Mel Martinez
Senator George S LeMieux
Senator Bill Nelson
Senator Marco Rubio
Congressman Cliff Stearns

- -

Ms. Leonnig also wrote, "The Kucheras have a complicated family history that involves drug-running and a family feud that left the brothers in control of the companies."

Dennis McGlynn, the company attorney who had conducted the sale, was mentioned in the article as saying that he thought I had known that I was selling the company to my nephews.

After this story was published, she called Mr. Dudiak, the alleged buyer of K.I.I., who told her he was never involved in the sale of the company. The excited reporter provided me with her phone number and email and asked me to call her back in a few days to complete the story. I called her two days later, and she informed me that she was no longer interested in this story. What had happened? It became obvious to me that the people who ran the paper did not want the truth to be revealed and that hiding Mr. Dudiak as a source made the crime less important.

Mr. Dudiak became so frightened that he called my nephew about it, so my nephew used the ten years of stolen government money and his attorney, Mr. John Eddy, an expensive lawyer, to send me a threatening letter about the accusations and the seriousness of the situation.

Throughout 2009, several newspaper articles were published about Murtha's alleged ties to my nephews and their company.[3]

Since I had left the company many years earlier, I had nothing to do with their dealings with Murtha. However, since my nephews and I share the same last name, reporters and government agencies always seemed to want to connect me with the company. A family feud with a shrewd uncle combined with a Congressional Ethics investigation of accusations of earmarks and political corruption always helps to propel a story.

Concurrently, I decided to employ Advantage Tax Inc. to represent me concerning my completely unrelated tax issue. I later learned they would not represent me in court until a ruling was made. However, they assured me that, after doing hundreds of this type of case, they never had a problem rectifying a situation like ours. My Attorney, Samantha Harris, advised me to get an extension. After several extensions, she told me the issue would be resolved in thirty days. However, sixty days later, she informed me that all their attempts to rectify my situation were being blocked by a technical service clerk, Steve Kovscek, out of the IRS office in Pittsburgh, PA. So, after I had paid them $4,800, Advantage Tax gave up on my case.

In their investigation of the IRS claim, my friend, Tax Attorney Jerry Rinzel, and all of my Certified Public Accountant friends could find nothing to support Steve Kovscek's actions. After checking my tax returns, they all determined that I owed nothing.

Only after Mr. Rinzel advised me to call the Taxpayer Advocacy Group for help in this matter was I made aware of a missing 1045 from my tax file. To remedy this situation, I completed a 1040X along with the 1045 to the IRS and a lengthy explanation from my tax attorney asking the IRS to inform him if they had any questions. Mr. Rinzel requested that any questions about the 1997 form 1040X be directed to him; however, none were raised. The fraudulent 1099 was never investigated.

Several months passed with no successful resolution. Finally, on November 12, 2009, they told me there was no 1045 form in my file. My contact person told me she had been taken off the case. Then, on November 14, 2009, my tax attorney pointed out that, in tiny print at the top of form 1045, the instructions indicated to put this form in a separate folder, which I did not do. He said they should have informed me of this error, which they did not. They had lost the document showing I owed no taxes for 1997.

On February 12, 2009, a lien was filed at the Ocala Federal Courthouse and was attached to all property I owned and any property I might acquire in the future. The person to contact about the lien was none other than Steven Kovscek.

It was also at this courthouse that I was asked to make some arrangements to collect the thirty thousand dollars overage monies that I had from the sheriff's sale of my house in a 2000 bankruptcy. As the judge instructed, I hired Attorney Tim Slone to represent me in collecting the money. The attorney didn't have the documents I sent him for this action, and the judge apparently became confused and put the money in an escrow fund until he could sort the problem out.

Steve Kovscek seemed obsessed with playing his cruel game and made yet another false accusation. A tax lien was filed at the Ebensburg Courthouse against my son, who has the same name as mine but a different social security number. On December 21, 2009, I spoke to the prothonotary office at the Cambria County Courthouse in Pennsylvania and asked who initiated this lien. They told me that Steve Kovscek, the clerk out of the Pittsburgh IRS office, had intervened, saying that the money belonged to the government. Later, when I asked the attorney to explain his reasoning, he simply said, "You can't fight the Feds."

I am beginning to think that there is some merit to that statement. After piecing together volumes of data that I collected in my years of searching, I now see the obvious evidence of a low-level IRS person. IRS agents were about to raid my old company, Kuchera Industries Inc. Out of that same IRS office, someone recognized my name and mistakenly thought I was somehow involved in the case they were pursuing.

Chapter 8: Health Issues

Various organizations under the environmentalism umbrella have been co-opted by fanatics who want to use ecological concerns to effect social engineering that was tried and failed under both fascist and communist regimes; many actually argue that human beings are "unnatural," an infection that is destroying the planet, and that we have no right to be here. — Dean Koontz, foreword to *Invasion of the Body Snatchers*

PHYSICALLY AND MENTALLY exhausted from our ordeals of losing the company that had once been my pride and joy and the constant roller coaster of financial turmoil, my wife and I both developed severe health issues. Our physical ailments were made worse because of the stress, uncertainty, utter devastation, and disappointment of how our family members duped us. This continuing twenty-year nightmare caused irreparable physiological and psychological damage to both of us.

I had developed a sciatic nerve problem from continuous driving, and it took a year for a chiropractor to rid me of a condition called drop foot. From then on, I have lived with a degenerating hip problem. Following my heart attack in 1997, two stents were placed in my heart arteries. My hip was replaced in January 2012, and I had a second heart issue on April 4, 2017.

My wife was suffering from a condition called trigeminal neuralgia. We traveled to Maryland every week for acupuncture so that she could have some relief. We eventually found help when a neurosurgeon used a gamma knife radio surgery ray to deaden the nerve, but after four years of this treatment, the condition vigorously re-surfaced. Now, the excruciating and debilitating pain could only be suppressed by taking a strong drug that could cause a seizure if it were stopped suddenly. She was already taking the maximum dosage.

Her condition became even worse after the summons on December 31, 2008. This single moment was truly an emotional blow to her, and to this day, she is perplexed at how someone could have the gall to serve a summons on New Year's Eve. Rosemarie's face was numb after a successful brain surgery in 2010, but now she is finally free from pain. However, the psychological damage and constant worry still continue to haunt both of us. She had a knee replacement on April 12, 2012.

Mentally, we both have been forced to live with the fact that what should have been the life of a successful businessman and his wife turned into over twenty years of angst—rummaging through documentation, searching for attorneys, communicating with representatives and congressmen, and frustratedly dwelling on the facts of why we were not able to resolve the wrongs that had been done to us.

Chapter 9: After Years of Searching

Whereby I do clearly collect thus much, that these adventures which we go in search of will bring us at last to so many disventures as we shall not be able to know which is our right foot. — Cervantes, *Don Quixote*

AFTER YEARS OF searching through multiple boxes of my files, I finally gathered all the evidence I thought I needed to prove my case and compiled the paperwork into a three-ring binder. When I think of the constant written and phone correspondence, I realize that my wife and I wasted years of our lives on this issue, which compounded the physical and mental strain amplified by our advanced age.

The incessant, senseless persecution from Steve Kovscek, an IRS clerk, who appeared to be going rabid to cover up the IRS's mistake, was exhausting. He had initiated every action taken against me. I finally connected the dots and found that I was a victim of a crime. The Pittsburgh office of the IRS had been investigating K.I.I., my old company, and although Mr. Kovscek was not part of that investigation team, he recognized my name.

After my ordeal with the IRS, I became curious and noticed a book, *Flat Tax Revolution: Using a Postcard to*

Abolish the IRS, by Steve Forbes.[4] I thought, "Wow! How can that be?" I began reading.

As I started to leaf through the book, I was immediately caught up in the early history of the United States and our early leaders' views on taxes. According to Forbes, Benjamin Franklin's quote, "In this world nothing can be said to be certain, except death and taxes," suggests that "Taxes are a certainty we dread almost as much as death" (Forbes, p. 1).

I am one of the millions of people who, every year, pay a fee for someone to navigate through the yearly tax booklet and let us know what we owe. We trust that they will do this job accurately and correctly. I never considered that we, the people, have the option of changing the system. We must get our representatives in the House and Senate interested in this plan.

I then began remembering our second president, John Adams, who spent his entire life trying to find a way to finance the newly formed government, and how he traveled to France and Holland to get a loan so the country could pay its debts. Then Thomas Jefferson joined the quest. In fact, Jefferson bought so many books when he was in France that he was basically bankrupt. Going through Forbes' book certainly got my ire up. Just think that, after all these years, the tax situation could have changed, but to this day, there is not enough support in Congress even to entertain the concept of a flat tax (Forbes, p. 78).

There are over a hundred thousand people working for the IRS. Most are just doing what is expected of them. However, in my case, one stepped out of his regular job and ventured into the outside world. He recognized my name and convinced himself to do something exciting, bringing the ten-year-old dead files to life.

Steve Kovscek knew that the IRS/FBI/ATF team was going to raid the company in January 2009. When he saw my name, he saw his opportunity to get in on the action and potentially make a name for himself. He underhandedly made me part of that raid with his last-minute New Year's Eve subpoena.

He committed a criminal act with the backing of hundreds of unsuspecting prosecuting attorneys. I tried to speak up for myself by calling and writing to four senators, the attorney General, and everyone else I could find. I had to borrow thousands of dollars to have a legal group defend me, but all of this was to no avail.

These are real crimes, and the proof is indisputable. Because of my name, I am now the victim of a crime. Because of my name, I am also a victim of a hate crime. We were pursued with extreme prejudice for no reason except a name. Because I had founded Kuchera Industries, my name was still connected with the company, even though I no longer had anything to do with it.

CHAPTER FOUR

Putting Johnstown Back On Track

ROAD TO RECOVERY

When we last visited Johnstown, Pennsylvania, we profiled local entrepreneurial heroes and town supporters. That was last year, when the town famous for its devastating floods began to blossom, thanks to its small-business community.

One year later, Johnstown continues to be plagued by the severe economic downturn created by the demise of its steel and coal industries. In fact, at press time, Bethlehem Steel Corp., the nation's second-largest steelmaker, announced plans to reduce its work force by 25 percent—a move that could cost Johnstown nearly 2,000 jobs, unless plans to sell Bethlehem Steel's Johnstown division goes through.

But while Johnstown struggles through the steel industry's worst slump in years, its small businesses are a beacon of hope. In this installment we focus on a key aspect of the community's economic revival that seems doubly appropriate to discuss during an election year: the federal government.

CAPITOL GAINS

In this time of recession, when many U.S. businesses are struggling for survival, small companies in the Johnstown area are winning the battle

Johnstown entrepreneurs Michael J. Kuchera Jr. (left) and Bill Kuchera prove you don't have to come from a big city to make it big—not if your town is behind you 100 percent.

to keep up with the overflow of work—largely due to strong support from Washington.

According to Bob Murphy, director of procurement technical assistance for Johnstown Area Regional Industries' (JARI) Defense Procurement Assistance Center (DPAC), 26 companies in the greater Johnstown area won 208 government contracts over the last year—either directly or on a subcontract basis with prime government contractors. That translates into $35.2 million for the Johnstown economy.

Founded in November 1990, DPAC assists companies in Pennsylvania's Cambria and Somerset counties that do military and other types of business with the federal

BY CHRISTINE FORBES

Epilogue

IT IS 2023, and the IRS is in the spotlight more than ever. Here I am writing this book to document my journey and my struggles to identify and expose, of all things, an IRS crime. I want to reach out to my readers and tell the truth about how I was needlessly dragged into the workings of a corrupt government employee. It was a hell of a ride, and now I am ready to share it with the world.

The nephews' crimes were rotten, but to have the federal government indulge in the activities that I detail in this book is serious and frightening as it involves taking away our freedoms. By stringing together multiple unrelated issues, the IRS created a false case that seemed real to anyone unfamiliar with my past.

As a citizen, I feel obligated to warn others to constantly monitor and understand the bookkeeping, logistics, and types of deals being made with other companies. Giving family members a chance to reform and putting trust in your friends is a beautiful thing, but proceed with caution and allow yourself to grasp the reality of the situation.

I have no regrets. As you may have gleaned from my background story, I enjoyed most of my working years. When I am not thinking about the havoc created by my nephews and the IRS, my wife and I are content with our lives in Florida. Writing this book has helped me to make sense of everything.

If this book helps one person avoid getting into a similar situation with the IRS, I have succeeded in my quest. Who knows? Perhaps in the future, someone in Congress will read about my ordeal and be convinced to change the tax laws so that individuals like me can succeed in business without fear of repercussions from the IRS.

Endnotes

1   https://www.tribdem.com/news/local_news/
federal-agencies-raid-kuchera-companies/article_d5acfc9d-18ee-50b6-aff9-
b86c830cd7a9.html

2   URL: https://www.washingtonpost.com/wp-dyn/content/arti-
cle/2009/07/07/AR2009070701129.html?hpid=moreheadlines

3   Open Source documents mentioning Murtha. https://vault.fbi.gov/
John%20Murtha/John%20Murtha%2015%20of%2032

4   Forbes, Steve. *Flat Tax Revolution: using a postcard to abolish the IRS.*
Washington DC: Regnery Publishing, Inc., 2005.

www.ingramcontent.com/pod-product-compliance
Lightning Source LLC
Chambersburg PA
CBHW022132280326
41933CB00007B/664